RIVERS THROUGH TIME

Settlements of the River
THAMES

Rob Bowden

Heinemann
LIBRARY

www.heinemann.co.uk/library
Visit our website to find out more information about Hei

To order:
☎ Phone 44 (0) 1865 888066
🖹 Send a fax to 44 (0) 1865 314091
💻 Visit the Heinemann Bookshop at www.heinemann.co.uk
catalogue and order online.

First published in Great Britain by Heinemann
Library, Halley Court, Jordan Hill, Oxford OX2 8EJ,
part of Harcourt Education.
Heinemann is a registered trademark of Harcourt
Education Ltd.

Editorial: Jilly Attwood and Kate Bellamy
Design: Richard Parker and
Tinstar Design Ltd (www.tinstar.co.uk)
Illustrator: Stephen Sweet and Jeff Edwards
Picture Research: Ruth Blair and Ginny Stroud-Lewis
Production: Séverine Ribierre
Originated by Dot Gradations Ltd
Printed in China by WKT Company Limited

ISBN 0 431 12042 0 (hardback)
09 08 07 06 05
10 9 8 7 6 5 4 3 2 1

ISBN 0 431 12047 1 (paperback)
10 09 08 07 06
10 9 8 7 6 5 4 3 2 1

British Library Cataloguing in Publication Data
Bowden, Rob
Settlements of the River Thames - (Rivers through
time)
942.2
A full catalogue record for this book is available from
the British Library.

Acknowledgements
The publishers would like to thank the following
for permission to reproduce photographs:
Alamy pp. 21 (Chris Andrews/Oxford Picture
Library), 8 (David Martyn Hughes), 12 (Image
Source), 13 (Nigel Reed), 29 (Oxford Picture Library);
Anglo Saxon Index at Trinity College,
Cambridge p. 11; Corbis p. 9 (Grant Smith);
Courtesy of Museum in Docklands, PLA Collection
pp. 15, 41; Hulton Deutsch p. 26; Maidenhead
Local History Archives p. 31, 33; Mary Evans
Picture Library p. 14; Oxfordshire Local Records
Office pp. 20, 23, 28, 37; Peter Evans pp. 4, 5, 17, 19,
22, 25, 35, 39, 42; Pictures of Britain p. 43;
Skyscan pp. 16, 27

Cover photograph reproduced with permission of
Corbis.

Disclaimer

Every effort has been made to contact copyright
holders of any material reproduced in this book. Any
omissions will be rectified in subsequent printings if
notice is given to the publishers.

The paper used to print this book comes from
sustainable resources.

Contents

Words in bold, **like this**, are explained in the Glossary.

Introducing the River Thames

A historical river

The Thames is by far the best known river in Britain, although it is not quite the longest (the River Severn is 10 kilometres, 6 miles, longer). The Thames flows through the heart of London, the capital city, and has played a central role in British history for some 2000 years. From the Roman invasions of 43 BC to the turn of the millennium in AD 2000, some of the most famous events in British history have taken place on or near the Thames. These include the signing of the **Magna Carta** in 1215, the plot to blow up the Houses of Parliament in 1605 and the Great Fire of London in 1666.

The Millennium Bridge is a modern crossing over the Thames in London. St Paul's Cathedral in the background is one of the Thames' most famous landmarks.

The historical importance of the Thames can be seen in the **settlements** that line its banks. Royal palaces, government buildings, great trading houses, market squares and river crossings all provide links with the past. Many of these settlements have changed little in hundreds of years. They are now the basis of a thriving tourist industry along the Thames that attracts millions of visitors every year.

The Thames is not just an historical river. Many people still depend on the river for their livelihoods, and humans continue to try to control and live with the Thames. As Britain enters the 21st century the relationship between the Thames and its people is changing again.

The Thames Flood Barrier opened in 1984. It was built to protect London from the high tides and flooding that affect the Thames in its lower reaches.

River terminology

Confluence – *the point where two rivers join.*

Delta – *where the river joins the sea.*

Mouth – *the ending point of a river.*

Reaches – *used to describe sections of the river (upper, middle and lower reaches).*

River course – *the path followed by a river from source to mouth.*

Source – *the starting point of a river.*

Tributary – *a river or stream that joins another (normally bigger) river.*

5

The Thames from source to mouth

In comparison with major rivers of the world, the Thames is a very small river. It has a total length of just 344 kilometres (213 miles). This compares to 3780 kilometres (2347 miles) for the Mississippi or 6650 kilometres (4130 miles) for the Nile, the world's longest river. Being such a short river, the Thames does not have the variety of features that are found in bigger rivers. It is slow and **meandering** for most of its length. At certain points, its meanders are so exaggerated that it nearly turns back on itself.

The source of the Thames is Thames Head, near the town of Cirencester. At an **altitude** of just 109 metres, in the corner of a meadow, lies a circle of stones. It is here that the Thames rises as a small spring. In all but the wettest of winters, however, the spring appears dry on the surface. This is because the young Thames runs underground and is not permanently visible until about a kilometre downstream.

The river runs from west to east, beginning life as a gentle stream winding slowly through the rolling countryside of the Cotswolds. It lies in a broad river valley dominated by **water meadows**, and collects water from various small streams and **tributaries** that swell the main channel. The Thames remains a fairly narrow river and by the time it reaches Oxford measures just 46 metres in width. Downstream of Oxford the sides of the river valley steepen as the Thames cuts through a line of chalk hills. This is known as the Goring Gap, the main physical feature on the river.

In its middle **reaches** the Thames continues in a series of giant meanders and widens slightly to around 76 metres at Teddington in London. At Teddington the Thames becomes a **tidal** river. This means it is influenced by the rise and fall of the tides, even though the North Sea is still 104 kilometres (65 miles) downstream. The Thames flows within **embankments** for much of its journey through London. The embankments were built to protect the city from the rise and fall of the river.

At its most extreme this tidal change can be as much as 7 metres. The Thames also widens gradually as it flows through London. By London Bridge, in the heart of the city, the river has reached a width of about 230 metres. As it leaves London and enters the Thames **estuary** the river widens more dramatically. By the time it joins the North Sea at the Nore (a sandbank running across the estuary) it is 9 kilometres (5½ miles) wide.

Map of the River Thames from its source at Thames Head near Cirencester to its mouth at the Thames Estuary.

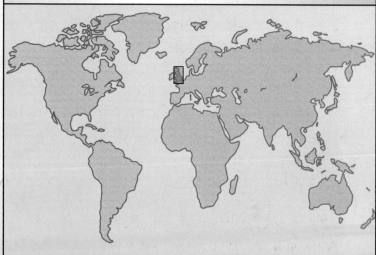

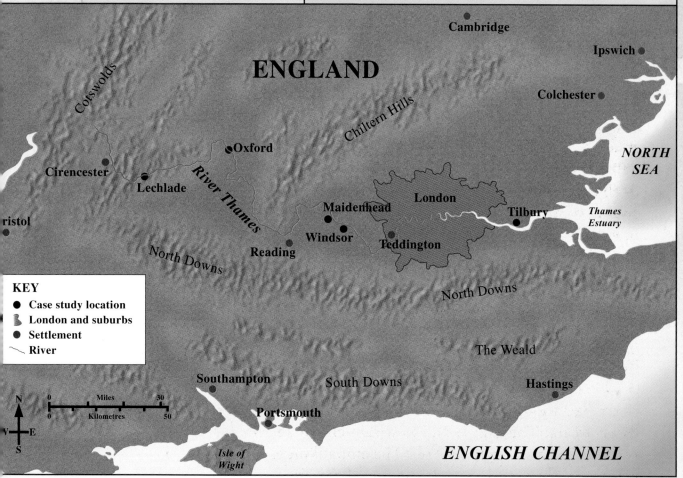

ENGLAND

Cambridge

Ipswich

Colchester

Cotswolds

Chiltern Hills

NORTH SEA

Oxford

Cirencester

River Thames

Lechlade

Bristol

Maidenhead

London

Tilbury

Thames Estuary

Windsor

Teddington

Reading

North Downs

North Downs

The Weald

KEY
● Case study location
🬀 London and suburbs
● Settlement
⌇ River

Southampton

South Downs

Hastings

Portsmouth

Miles 0 — 30
Kilometres 0 — 50

N
W—E
S

Isle of Wight

ENGLISH CHANNEL

Settlements of the Thames

The settlements along the Thames vary enormously. In its upper reaches, most settlements are little more than villages or small towns inhabited by just a few thousand people. This part of the river remains much as it has for thousands of years and the land to either side is still mainly farmland. It is popular with tourists who want to escape from the cities and enjoy the countryside.

The River Thames flows through rural areas, like Berkshire, as well as cities.

What's in a name?

Some people think that the name Thames derives from the Sanskrit word tamas, *meaning dark, which could describe the dark, cloudy waters of the river. Another theory is that it is based on the Roman words* tam, *meaning 'wide', and* isis, *meaning 'water', as 'Tamesis' or 'Tamesa' were former names for the Thames. (In Oxford the Thames is still known as the Isis as it passes through the city.) Or the name may come from the Old English verbs 'te' or 'ta', meaning 'to flow'. Many other rivers in Britain and Europe are believed to share this origin.*

A road bridge at Dartford on the outskirts of London crosses the Thames as it enters the Thames estuary. The river is wide and slow-moving at this point.

In its middle section the Thames passes through several larger settlements such as Oxford and Reading. These cities were first established as crossing points over the Thames but now extend along the river for several kilometres before the countryside again takes over.

By Maidenhead, the Thames is becoming an increasingly **urban** river, with only pockets of countryside remaining. From here the Thames passes through the most built-up and populated part of the UK.

London is by far the biggest settlement along the Thames and is home to almost 8 million people. As it carves its way through the heart of the city, the river provides a focus for city life. The riverfront is a mix of the historical and the ultra-modern, reflecting London's changes and developments.

This book will explore some of the better-known settlements along the Thames. It follows a passage through time, starting with the foundation of London nearly 2000 years ago and ending with Tilbury, the modern Thames port. We will consider why settlements formed where they did and what role the river played in their foundation. We will look at how settlements have changed over time, what the future may hold for them, and about the changing role of the Thames itself in the lives of the people living alongside it.

London: a capital with history

Roman London

When the Romans invaded Britain in AD 43, the site that is now London was little more than a swampy river marsh. The Thames formed a natural barrier between the Roman landing points on the south coast of England and the most important **settlement** of the time, Colchester, to the north of the Thames. To overcome this problem the Romans built a wooden bridge across the Thames in AD 50. The crossing point was carefully chosen, as this was where seagoing ships could anchor in the **tidal** waters of the Thames. It enabled the Romans to use the Thames as a route for transporting goods between Rome, the capital of the empire, and their new **province** of Britannia (the Roman name for Britain). They built a small port to handle the goods, and the settlement of Londinium (London) soon formed.

In AD 60 Londinium was destroyed by the invasion of Queen Boudica, a leader from a tribe living in what are now the English counties of Norfolk and Suffolk. She led a rebellion against the Romans, but the Roman forces were too powerful and regained control the following year. The Roman emperor sent a civilian administrator named Julius Classicianus to rebuild Londinium as a planned Roman settlement. It quickly became a centre for trade, with the Thames at its centre.

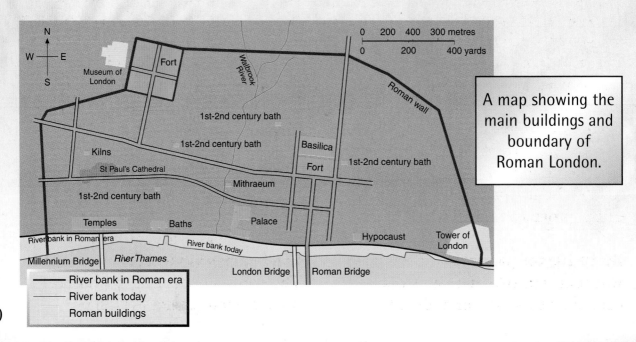

A map showing the main buildings and boundary of Roman London.

FACT

Coins found in the Thames riverbed show that Londinium had its own coin **mint** and was the financial centre of Roman Britain.

Goods arriving in Londinium were vital for supplying the armies of the Roman Empire and allowing them to expand their control in Britain. **Wharves** were built along the river to handle goods as they were transported between Londinium and Rome. The Romans also built a network of roads to link the Thames to other important settlements such as Chester, York and Colchester. By AD 100, Londinium was the capital of the province of Britannia.

By AD 200 the province of Britannia was split into two, with a second capital in York, so Londinium lost some of its political importance. It remained a vital commercial centre, however, with the Thames at the centre of its trade. Glass, pottery, lead and silver were among the goods made or traded in Londinium at this time. **Archaeologists** have found evidence that shows how the Romans improved the riverfront using timber to create artificial **embankments** along the river's edge to allow ships to dock and unload their cargoes. However, in around AD 410 Roman rule in Britain came to an end and Londinium was virtually abandoned. The port and river traffic fell into decline – though not for long.

The rise of a capital

The **Saxons** arrived in Britain in around AD 450. Upon reaching the Thames they settled slightly to the west of Roman Londinium and formed a settlement called Ludenwic. Like the Romans, the Saxons saw how important the Thames would be for trade with the outside world. They continued to build riverside embankments and to improve port facilities for seagoing ships. Archaeologists in Britain have unearthed pottery from France, coins from Belgium and ornate Scandinavian metalwork from this period showing that the Thames was already at the centre of international trade in Europe.

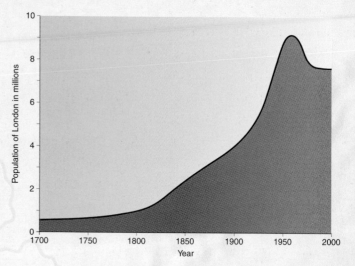

London's population continued to grow dramatically until the second half of the Twentieth century.

The Houses of Parliament in Westminster, London. The centre of power in Britain has been here for over 800 years.

By the 9th century London was fast becoming the wealthiest settlement in England, though the capital was Winchester. The river traffic brought great wealth to the city and made London a major target for invading forces. Control of the city changed hands several times until King Canute finally brought some stability to the city in 1016. It was King Canute who built the Palace of Westminster on the site where the Houses of Parliament now stand. He also began to transfer greater powers from Winchester to London. London finally became the capital city in the mid-12th century and continued to thrive as a trade centre.

By the reign of Elizabeth I (1588–1603) the Thames waterfront was so busy that there was not enough space for all the ships wishing to dock. Smaller boats called **lighters** were used to offload ships anchored in the Thames and transport their goods to less crowded parts of the riverbank. This led to the expansion of London along the riverfront – a process that continued until the mid-20th century.

This monument, near London Bridge, commemorates the Great Fire of London.

The Great Fire of London

On 2 September 1666 a fire broke out in a bakers in Pudding Lane, near London Bridge. Strong wind caused the fire to spread quickly through the wooden buildings of the time. Over the next three days the fire destroyed almost 80 per cent of the city. The river was one of the main escape routes during the fire. By the time the fire finally died down on 5 September, some 100,000 Londoners had been made homeless and Thames-side London lay in ruins.

The world's busiest port

During the 17th and 18th centuries, ships became larger and traders explored ever more distant shores. They brought back goods such as cotton, tea, spices, ivory, wine, rum, fruit and dyes. The Thames remained the main destination for offloading these cargoes, so London's importance grew. In the late 18th century the **Industrial Revolution** began in England and turned the nation into a major manufacturing centre. The Thames became one of the main routes for bringing raw materials into England and transporting finished goods to foreign markets. By the early 19th century some shipping companies began to build their own docks to handle the increase in river traffic. Large areas of London were cleared to make way for these docks. When St Katherine's Dock was built in the 1820s for example, 11,000 people were forced to move as some 1250 houses and a 12th-century church were knocked down.

This drawing of a textile mill on the River Thames from the early 19th century, shows how important the river was for powering industry as well as transporting its produce.

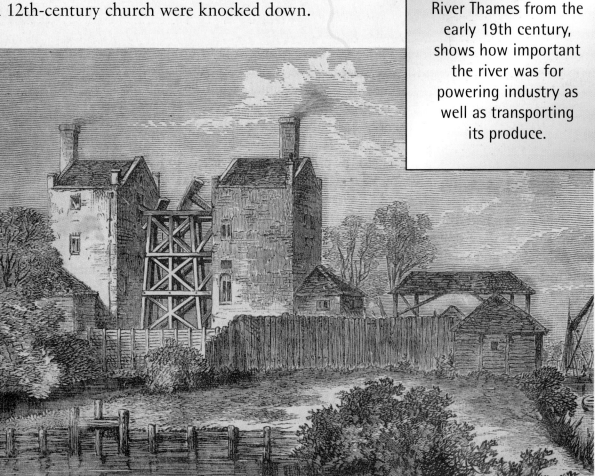

Goods being loaded onto ships in the London docklands in the 1930s.

Before the docks were built it took 7–14 days to unload a 350-ton ship from the riverbank. The docks cut this time dramatically. St Katherine's Dock could offload a 250-ton ship in just 12 hours and could turn around a 500-ton vessel in just 2–3 days. The new docks were an instant success and helped turn London into the world's busiest port. The docks were extended in the mid-1800s as they again struggled to cope with the volume of trade. The last of these docks was King George V Dock, which was opened in 1921.

Life in the docks

Dock work was poorly paid and the constant movement of heavy goods meant it was often dangerous too. Most dock workers (dockers) were employed as casual labourers when ships arrived for unloading, and then laid off when the docks were empty. On one day a dock may have needed 3000 men and on the next only 200. Dockers worked in gangs of around a dozen men, often with relatives, to look out for each other's safety. 'Stevedores' were the most skilled workers in the docks. It was their job to carefully load ships so that they would not capsize and lose their precious cargo at sea.

A century of change

In the early 20th century London continued to grow around the trade of the Thames. The London docklands suffered severe bomb damage during the Second World War (1939–45), but recovered to handle more goods than ever by the early 1960s. By 1968, however, three of London's major docks had closed and over the next twenty years most of the other docks were shut and thousands of jobs lost.

Dramatic change in the way cargo was handled was mostly to blame for these dock closures. Beginning in the late 1960s, goods were packed in standard-sized **containers** that could be transported by road or rail and easily transferred between ships, trucks and trains. This removed the need for dockside warehouses and made the unloading of ships a completely mechanical task. These container ships were also much bigger than earlier ships had been and needed deep-water **berths** in order to dock and unload. London's ageing docklands could not provide these facilities and so lost much of their trade to newer coastal ports.

Viewed from the air, the Thames winds through the heart of London like a giant snake.

AD50	100	1666
Wooden bridge is built across the Thames by the Romans.	Londinium is capital of Britannia.	Great Fire of London, lasting 3 days.

Office blocks dominate the redeveloped Canary Wharf in London's docklands.

In the 1980s the government launched plans to redevelop the Thames docks. The London Docklands Development Corporation (LDDC) was formed to manage the redevelopment and to attract new businesses into the docklands. After twenty years of building work the docklands are once again a thriving riverside community. The river is today more of an attractive setting than a commercial waterway. The old docks now house yachts and pleasure craft instead of seagoing ships. What were once warehouses are today luxury apartments, offices or shops. There are many new developments too, such as the Canary Wharf office complex and the Docklands Arena.

FACT

The tower at Canary Wharf is the tallest building in Britain and the second highest in Europe at 248 metres.

By the time the LDDC finished its redevelopment of the docklands in 1998 the area had been completely transformed. Over 24,000 new homes had been built and some 2700 new businesses located themselves there, providing over 85,000 jobs. Although many things have changed since London was founded, one thing has remained the same – the close ties between the city, its people and the River Thames.

1939-1945	1968	1980s
Second World War badly damages London's docklands.	Three of London's major docks closed.	Government plans to redevelop the abandoned docks along the Thames in London are launched.

Oxford: a university city

Ancient crossing place

Oxford is best known for its university. The 39 colleges and more than 15,000 students that make up Oxford University dominate the city. Some of the colleges date back to the 13th century. The origins of Oxford date back further, however, to a legendary **Saxon** princess and nun called Frideswide. She is said to have founded a monastery in about AD 700 close to a crossing point in the Thames. This crossing point, or 'ford' was used for taking oxen across the river. It is the combination of the words 'oxen' and 'ford' that give Oxford its name.

By the 9th century, records show that Oxford had become an important market town, benefiting from its location at the river crossing, and also as the point where the Thames is joined by the River Cherwell – one of its major **tributaries**. At the time, these rivers would have been one of the only forms of transport.

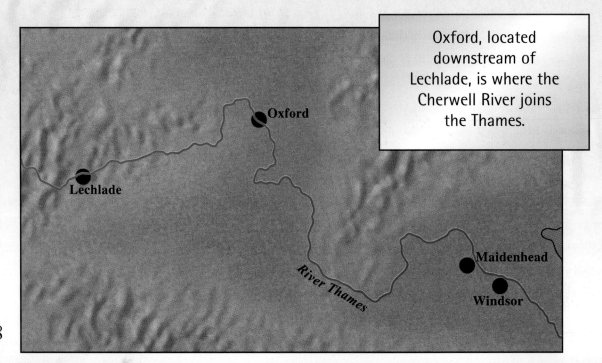

Oxford, located downstream of Lechlade, is where the Cherwell River joins the Thames.

Folly Bridge was the first bridge to be built across the Thames in Oxford. It is very near the point where the original oxen ford is believed to have been.

Of great importance to the early growth of Oxford was its location on the border between two Saxon kingdoms. Wessex lay to the south of the Thames whilst Mercia was to the north of the river. Oxford became a centre of trade between the two kingdoms and grew rapidly during this time. The Saxon period came to an end in 1014 following their defeat by Viking forces from Denmark. By this time Oxford was so important that the Danish King Canute chose to hold his coronation (crowning ceremony) in the city in 1018.

Royal escape

*In 1142 the Thames in Oxford became the subject of a famous escape by Empress Matilda (daughter of King Henry I). Between 1135 and 1148 Matilda was involved in a **civil war** with King Stephen over her right to the throne of England. In 1141 she went to London to be crowned as queen, but was chased back to Oxford by supporters loyal to the King. The following year she was **besieged** in Oxford Castle by King Stephen. Rather than surrender, Matilda made a daring escape during a snowstorm by climbing down the walls of the castle and crossing the ice-covered Thames. By dressing in white she was able to camouflage herself against the snow and escape unseen.*

A working river

In the mid 13th century, religious scholars in Oxford founded several colleges in the town. These later became the University of Oxford, attracting students from all over Europe. The student population created a new demand for goods and services. Many of the goods they needed were transported to Oxford up the Thames and unloaded at the city **wharves**. Craftsmen soon recognized the valuable market for their goods in Oxford and began to move to the town. By the late 13th century, Oxford had numerous cottage industries to supply the university scholars. These included furniture-makers, saddlers, shoemakers, weavers and brewers. Oxford became particularly well known for its cloth and leather. Both industries use large amounts of water to help prepare, soften and clean the cloth or leather and the Thames provided a reliable source of water for these processes.

The university's need for books led to the development of an important new industry in Oxford – printing and publishing. The first book to be printed in Oxford dates back to 1478. It was almost two centuries later, however, before the industry became properly established.

Wharf cranes, like this one, helped unload goods that had been transported to Oxford up the Thames.

The University of Oxford's buildings dominate the city and stretch down to the banks of the Thames.

Publishing created a demand for paper and several paper mills were built along the Thames to meet this demand. The mills used the power of the Thames to drive the machinery for making paper.

In 1790 the Thames at Oxford entered a new phase in its development with the completion of the Oxford canal. This artificial waterway linked Oxford and other **settlements** of the Thames to the industrial heartland of the Midlands. In particular it allowed coal to be transported directly from the Midlands to Oxford rather than via London and the Thames. The canal greatly boosted riverside activity in Oxford. At the start of the 20th century the Oxford canal was carrying some 450,000 tons of goods a year.

During the late 19th century, however, the Thames had begun to decline in importance as a transport route. The railways arrived in Oxford in 1843 and gradually replaced the river as the favoured method of transportation. Industries also became less reliant on the river, as coal, and later electricity, replaced water as a source of power. This enabled factories to be built away from the river and by the mid-20th century the Thames had all but ceased to be a working river in Oxford.

Pleasure on the Thames

Today the Thames in Oxford is used mainly for pleasure and recreation rather than for industry. On a summer day the river and its banks are buzzing with life. Christ Church meadow, where the Cherwell joins the Thames, is especially popular for walking along the riverbank, but boating remains the real attraction of the Thames.

An unusual form of boat in Oxford is the flat-bottomed punt. Punts would originally have been used by local ferry men to carry goods and passengers on the river. Today they are popular with students and tourists who can have a go themselves or pay to be chauffeured in style.

Punts provide a relaxing way for tourists to experience life on the Thames in Oxford.

700	**1018**	**1142**
Frideswide founds a monastery near the oxen ford.	King Canute is crowned in Oxford.	Empress Matilda is besieged by King Stephen and escapes from Oxford Castle.

Ornate college barges once provided Thames-side viewing platforms for watching the Univerity of Oxford's world-famous rowing teams.

Oxford rowing

*Rowing on the Thames at Oxford dates back to the late 1700s when it was a popular student leisure and exercise activity. In 1815 two college crews raced home after a day on the river. With eight men in each boat, the race soon became an annual event known as the 'Eights'. By 1840 fourteen colleges competed in the eights. Rowing became firmly established as the university's main sport. Many colleges purchased ornate **barges**, moored along the Thames, to use as club houses and viewing platforms. These have now been replaced by permanent club houses on the land. The biggest race is when Oxford take on their rival university, Cambridge, in the university boat race. This takes place annually on a section of the Thames further downstream in London. In 2004 Cambridge won the 150th boat race and overall Cambridge wins by to 78 to 71. There was one dead heat in 1877.*

Thames cruises are also popular. They take tourists up and down a short stretch of the river as it passes through Oxford. In the 19th century similar cruises were made in houseboats that were pulled along the riverbank by teams of horses. Steamboats also offered river cruises, some of which went as far as London, with overnight stops along the way.

1300s	1478	1790	1843
Religious scholars found the first colleges in Oxford.	Book printing begins in Oxford.	Oxford canal is completed.	Railways arrive in Oxford.

Windsor: a royal city

Royal waters

Connections between the Thames and royalty go back hundreds of years, but nowhere are they more obvious than in Windsor. A small town, on a bend in the river, Windsor is dominated by its splendid castle. It is one of the finest **medieval** castles in England and has been a royal residence for over 900 years. Indeed the castle is the reason for the **settlement** existing at all and dates back to the time of William I (William the Conqueror).

William I became king of England in 1066 after defeating King Harold in the Battle of Hastings. On surveying his new kingdom, William identified a chalk **bluff** on a bend of the Thames. Only a day's march from London, an excellent defensive lookout and with river connection to London for trade and supplies, it was an ideal location for a fort. The first fort, built in about 1070 on what was then known as Clewer Hill, would have been a simple wooden structure with defensive ditches. The first stone parts were erected around one hundred years later. The castle has been added to, restored and adapted ever since.

> Windsor began as a fort built by William I on a bend of the River Thames.

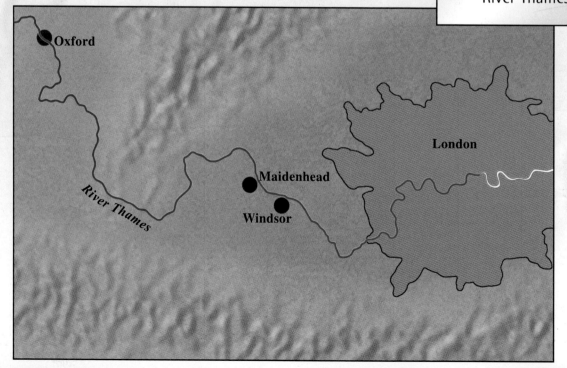

Origins of a name

*It is said that Windsor may get its name from a windlass (**winch**) that would have been used to tow the **barges** upstream from London, against the current of the river. Other accounts suggest that the name comes more directly from the Thames and an older name Windlesora, meaning 'the winding shores' of the river in this stretch. Whichever is true it seems clear that the Thames played a major role in the naming of Windsor.*

As the castle grew in size and importance so did the settlement around it. The castle needed supplies, many of which were brought in by river and unloaded at **wharves** along the riverfront. In time, a market town developed to meet the castle's needs and to trade by river with London.

Trade was further boosted when a wooden bridge was constructed across the Thames. The first bridge may have been built as early as the 12th century, but it has been rebuilt many times since then. The iron bridge that still stands today was built in 1824.

Windsor is dominated by its impressive castle, which stands guard over the Thames below.

Naturally vulnerable

The Thames has dominated Windsor ever since its founding. The river in this section regularly floods, so low-lying land along the river has never been built on. In years of especially high rainfall, however, the Thames has often flooded large areas of Windsor and its neighbouring settlements. Flooding was probably one of the major reasons for the continual rebuilding of the wooden bridge that connects Windsor with Eton, on the opposite bank.

Some of the worst floods in Windsor have occurred in its more recent history. Between 1869 and 2000, for example, there were fourteen major floods. One of the worst floods recorded in Windsor was in 1947. In March of that year, during an unusually cold winter, ground was too frozen for the heavy rain to sink in, so it ran off the surface into the Thames. Water levels in Windsor rose to around 2 metres higher than normal.

The flooding in Windsor in 1947. If these floods were to happen today they would affect 5500 properties, 12,500 people and cause damage worth about £40 million.

This graph shows the years (at the top) in which Windsor has experienced its most serious floods.

Major Thames floods at Windsor

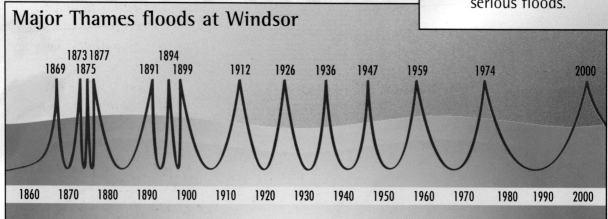

| 1869 | 1873 1877 1875 | 1891 | 1894 1899 | 1912 | 1926 | 1936 | 1947 | 1959 | 1974 | 2000 |

| 1860 | 1870 | 1880 | 1890 | 1900 | 1910 | 1920 | 1930 | 1940 | 1950 | 1960 | 1970 | 1980 | 1990 | 2000 |

Hundreds of properties were badly flooded, and many people were trapped in their homes. The army was brought in to help the townsfolk and limit the damage. They got rid of trees upstream and any boats that came adrift from their moorings, to prevent them being carried away by the river and colliding with the town's bridge.

In Windsor many families were evacuated by boats and taken to higher ground. Boats were also used to deliver milk and other supplies – even hot meals. People trapped in their homes used ropes and hooks to hoist supplies up to their first floor windows from boats below. The flooding led to an international appeal to help the people of Windsor rebuild their homes and lives. Luckily, since the castle stands on high ground, it was saved from the damaging floods.

> The Jubilee River is an artificial channel 11 km (7 miles) long that protects Windsor from flooding.

Living with risk

The residents of Windsor have learned how to live with the risk of flooding. Following the 1947 flood new guidelines were introduced to control building on land known to be vulnerable to flooding. More recently (2001) a diversion scheme called the Jubilee River was completed. This artificial channel can be used to divert some of the Thames' water when the river is in flood. In January 2003 the Jubilee River was used for the first time to carry around 40 per cent of the Thames' flow. It proved a great success, protecting around 1400 properties from flooding.

Tourist hot spot

The combination of history, royalty and the Thames have helped to make Windsor one of Britain's most popular tourist destinations. The Royal Borough of Windsor and its neighbouring town of Maidenhead welcome some seven million visitors every year. At least 11,000 people are employed in the tourism industry and many others benefit from visitors coming to the town. Windsor Castle alone attracts almost a million visitors a year.

FACT

Windsor castle has long been a favourite residence of the Royal family. In 1917 King George V liked it so much that he changed his family surname to Windsor.

Tourism started in Windsor during Victorian times when the railway made Windsor easily accessible from London. On summer weekends the banks of the Thames would be crowded and the river came to life with hundreds of rowing boats.

The Thames at Windsor was a lively riverside scene in Victorian times.

1070	1824	1917
William I builds the first fort at Windsor.	Iron bridge is built across the Thames at Windsor.	King George V changes his surname to Windsor.

Swan upping

In the third week of July each year an event called swan upping takes place on the Thames. It dates back to the 12th century, when all swans along this stretch of the Thames became the property of the monarch unless otherwise marked. Swans were highly prized as food for banquets and feasts, and swan upping allowed the monarch to put their mark on any unmarked swans. In the 15th century two other companies, the Vintners and the Dyers, were granted rights to own swans, so they marked their swans differently to the monarch. The Vintners marked their swans by scratching a pattern on one side of the bill, and the Dyers marked the other side. Swan upping continues today as an annual check on the population of Thames' swans. Traditional boats decorated with flags process slowly upstream. As they pass through Romney Lock, closest to Windsor Castle, the swan uppers stand in the boats and make a toast to the monarch of the day, a reminder of the historic links between royalty and the Thames.

Steam cruises brought more visitors, with regular services running between Oxford (upstream) and Kingston (downstream). The height of the Thames as a tourist attraction may have passed, but it remains one of the most popular ways to see Windsor. From the river it is easy to see the important location of Windsor and appreciate why William I chose to build a fort there.

1947	2001	2003
One of the worst floods in Windsor.	Jubilee River diversion scheme is completed.	Jubilee River is used for the first time.

Maidenhead: the crossroads

Crossing the Thames

Evidence of **settlements** in and around Maidenhead dates back to Roman times. The current town was founded in around 1250, when a wooden bridge was built across the Thames. This attracted traders, who took advantage of the business brought by the new crossing. The building of a new **wharf** near to the bridge in around 1297 brought trade from the Thames itself. This allowed boats from other settlements along the Thames, such as London, Windsor, Reading and Oxford, to land at Maidenhead. The wharf's importance is reflected in the name of the town. The **Saxon** for a wharf was 'hythe', and 'maiden' refers to something new. Together they form 'maiden-hythe', which became 'Maidenhead'.

Although river transport on the Thames was a feature of Maidenhead's growth it was the river crossing that was of greater significance. The bridge formed the vital link on the main land route between London and Bristol – two of the country's major ports. This led to Maidenhead developing into an important **coaching town**. Coaching became the main economic activity of the town between the 16th and mid-19th centuries. Coaching inns provided accommodation and food for the horsemen and their weary travellers.

> Maidenhead first developed as a landing point for boats travelling south-west along the Thames.

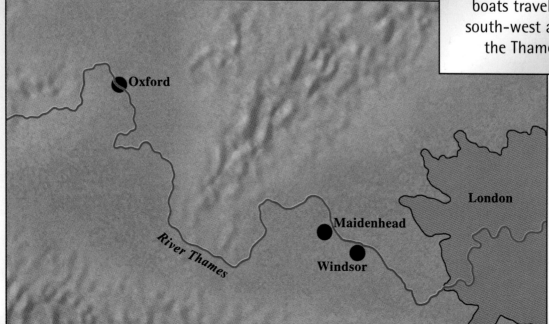

They also had stables to look after the needs of the horses. Maidenhead probably reached its peak as a coaching town during the 18th century. Over 90 coaches a day would pass through the town, making it one of the busiest coaching stops in the country. A new stone **toll** bridge was built across the Thames in 1777 to cope with the increased demand. This bridge still stands, though the toll was stopped in 1903.

The introduction of the railways during the 19th century saw the coaching era come to an end.

Maidenhead remained an important river crossing, however. In 1839 a new bridge was built by the famous engineer Isambard Kingdom Brunel to carry the Great Western Railway across the Thames. The railway brought London within easy reach, and Maidenhead quickly became a popular destination for Londoners wishing to escape the city. They came to Maidenhead to enjoy a relaxing day on the Thames. This popularity continues today, with Maidenhead being one of the busiest stretches of the river for pleasure craft.

This is the stone toll bridge in Maidenhead built in 1777 as a result of the large number of coaches passing through the town daily.

A mill town

Maidenhead became a significant centre for the milling industry. Water wheels in the mills used the moving water to power mill machinery. Flour milling was particularly important and continued in the town until around 1920. Most mills closed down as new forms of energy, such as coal and electricity, developed. Many mills were demolished, but some have been converted into luxury homes. In Maidenhead, the old flour mill is now a popular hotel called Boulters Inn. Boulter is an old milling term for a sieve that separates the bran from the flour. The name keeps alive the historic link with milling on the Thames at Maidenhead.

One mill that still survives today is Taplow Paper Mill. It produces corrugated paper for making cardboard boxes. The mill uses water from the Thames to help cool machinery used in the production process. Some water is also used to make pulp as part of the paper-making process, but the water that is only used for cooling is returned to the Thames.

A cross section of a water mill. The running water turns the water wheel, and powers the mill to grind grain into flour.

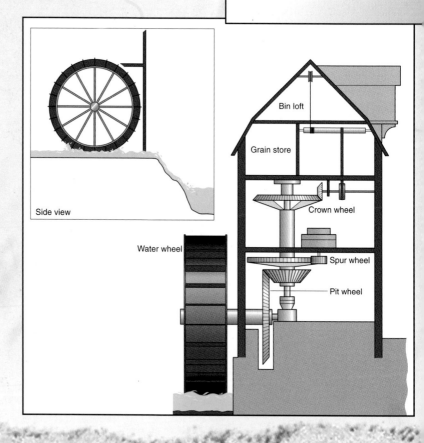

Side view

Water wheel

Bin loft

Grain store

Crown wheel

Spur wheel

Pit wheel

1250

Founding of Maidenhead, with wooden bridge built across the Thames.

1297

Wharf built near Maidenhead's bridge, bringing in trade.

River, rail and road

The Thames in Maidenhead is now mainly used for pleasure boating. Its days as a major transport link to London ended with the development of the railways. The railways are still running and Brunel's bridge is one of the most important in the UK, providing a vital link between London and the west. Today, however, the motorway network is the major transport link. The M4 motorway crosses the Thames on the outskirts of Maidenhead. These good transport links have attracted new businesses to Maidenhead, and housing has been built to accommodate more workers. Whilst few of them have anything to do with the river today, they all owe their success to that original crossing point over the Thames.

> Brunel's railway bridge across the Thames at Maidenhead has the widest and flattest brick-built arches in the world. It is known as the 'Sounding Arch Bridge' because of the way echoes travel around its enormous arches.

1777	1839	c1920
A new stone toll bridge is built across the Thames at Maidenhead.	Brunel's 'Sounding Arch Bridge' is built across the Thames.	Flour milling stops in Maidenhead.

Lechlade: the head of navigation

A market town

Lechlade is a small market town dating back to the early 13th century. It benefits from its position as the highest point of **navigation** on the Thames (the highest point that boats can travel to). Because it is close to the river's source, the river upstream of Lechlade becomes too narrow and shallow for most boats. **Wharves** were built at Lechlade to transfer goods between the river and land, so that they could continue their onward journey.

Over time, Lechlade became a centre for transporting Cotswold goods downstream to London. Wool, Cotswold stone and Gloucester cheese were particularly prized and became a focus of activity in and around the village. It was from Lechlade that some of the stone used to rebuild St Paul's Cathedral in London (1675–1710) was taken. Wool was especially valuable, bringing great wealth to Lechlade. Many of the grand houses and churches of the region were built from the proceeds of the wool trade.

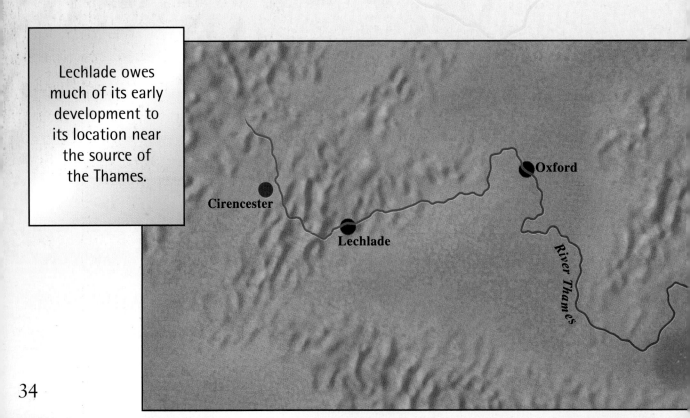

Lechlade owes much of its early development to its location near the source of the Thames.

Cirencester

Oxford

Lechlade

River Thames

These industries have now declined, but Lechlade remains as a gathering point for **narrow boats** and cruise boats as they reach the furthest point in the river. In addition, its old wharf has become a centre for tourist trips on the river and the hiring of boats.

In the town itself, many former trading stores are now restaurants or gift shops, designed to meet the demands of tourists. The river is still at the heart of the town, but the nature of its use has changed dramatically.

Halfpenny Bridge

*In Lechlade's early days the Thames would have been crossed by ferry or by a ford close to the present-day wharf. A stone bridge (St John's bridge) about a mile downstream was built in 1229, but Lechlade had to wait almost another 600 years before getting its own bridge. Halfpenny (pronounced 'haypnee') Bridge was built in 1792 and is still used today. Its high central arch allows barges to pass underneath without needing to lower their masts. The name of the bridge comes from the **toll** (half a penny) that was once charged to cross it. The tolls were stopped in 1839 for foot passengers and around 1885 for farmers herding cattle.*

Canal junction

Lechlade's significance as a transportation centre increased dramatically in 1789 when a canal linking it with the River Severn was completed. The Thames and Severn Canal took six and a half years to build and linked together England's two most important waterways at the time. It made water transportation possible between London and Bristol and was used to transport coal from the Midlands to London.

Locks

A lock is a device used on rivers or canals that allows boats to be raised or lowered from one water level to another. The main feature of a lock is the chamber, which has gates that can be opened and closed at either end. The water in the chamber is controlled by opening or shutting paddles. Once the boat reaches the correct level the gates are opened for it to continue its journey either up- or downstream.

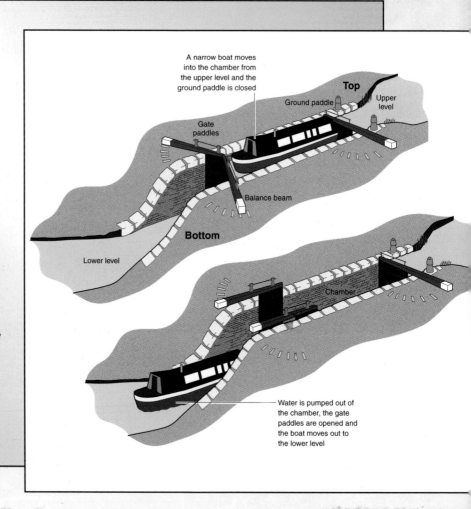

A narrow boat moves into the chamber from the upper level and the ground paddle is closed

Top

Ground paddle

Upper level

Gate paddles

Balance beam

Bottom

Lower level

Chamber

Water is pumped out of the chamber, the gate paddles are opened and the boat moves out to the lower level

---

1229

St John's bridge is built a mile downstream from Lechlade.

1789

Lechlade canal link to the River Severn is completed.

St John's Lock, near Lechlade, is the highest lock on the Thames and also one of its first.

Building the Thames and Severn Canal involved some major engineering challenges, including digging a tunnel through the limestone hills of the Cotswolds. When it was finished, the Sapperton Tunnel, as it was called, was the longest canal tunnel in Britain, at 3490 metres. It has since been overtaken by two others.

The Thames and Severn Canal joins the Thames just upstream of Lechlade. Lechlade itself became a thriving centre for the movement of coal, and the town and river both prospered as a result. Unfortunately, errors in the design and building of the canal meant that it suffered water shortages almost as soon as it opened. Despite efforts to prevent water loss and improve navigation with the construction of several locks, the Canal lost custom to newer canals opening closer to London. These included the Oxford and Grand Junction canal. The introduction of the railways further reduced the importance of the Thames and Severn Canal and by the end of the 19th century it had closed.

Attempts were made to restore and revive the canal, but it was finally abandoned around 1930 and remains closed today.

1792	1930
Halfpenny Bridge is constructed at Lechlade.	Lechlade canal is abandoned.

Tilbury: gateway to the Thames

Defending the capital

Archaeological evidence suggests that Tilbury has been an important **settlement** since Roman times. Its name, however, is thought to have originated later, during **Saxon** times. 'Tilla' was the name of a local chieftain whilst 'burg' was the Saxon term for a fort. Like many place names, 'Tilla-burg' changed over time to become Tilbury.

The origins of Tilbury as a fort are not surprising given its position. It is located at a point where the Thames **estuary** narrows before heading upstream to London. This makes it a perfect place to defend the river from enemy ships and prevent attacks on London. As a result, much of Tilbury's history has been as a military fort. Henry VIII built one of the first forts at Tilbury in 1539–40. Fearing a Spanish invasion following his divorce from Catherine of Aragon, he built a number of **blockhouses**, each armed with 25–30 artillery guns – but the invasion never came. The blockhouses were put into action in 1588, however, during the invasion of the Spanish Armada.

Tilbury is located on a narrow stretch of the Thames estuary.

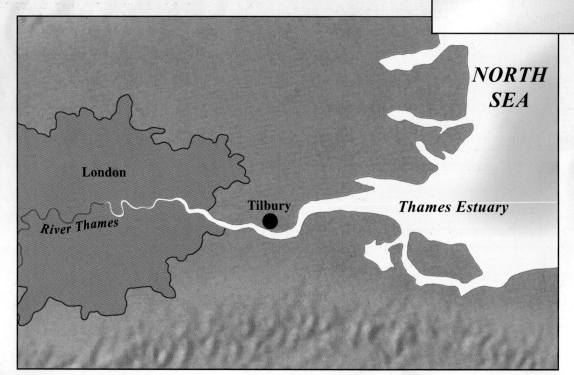

London

River Thames

Tilbury

Thames Estuary

NORTH SEA

Before the battle, some 12,000 troops camped out on Tilbury marshes next to the fort. They were visited by Queen Elizabeth I, who gave a famous speech to prepare them for the battle ahead.

The fort at Tilbury was again active during an invasion by the Dutch in 1667, but the Dutch turned back because they thought that the fort was too well armed. In fact the ageing fort was in a poor state of repair and the government realized that it must build a new one if it was to continue protecting London from attacks. Between 1670 and 1684, a pentagonal (five-sided) fort with a double moat was constructed. It was so well built that it still stands on the site today and has hardly changed. In the event, the fort was never actually attacked, but because of the importance of protecting London and the Thames it remained a military **garrison** until 1920. Today the fort is managed by English Heritage as a tourist attraction. Its conservation provides a permanent reminder of Tilbury's importance in defending the Thames.

Tilbury has modern dock facilities for transferring container cargo quickly between ships and road or rail.

Tilbury docks

Tilbury's growth can be traced back to the decision by the **East and West India Dock Company** to build a new dock there in 1886. The area was ideal for a dock, as it had plenty of flat land, deep water for allowing even the largest of ships to dock, and a rail connection with London. Although it was some 25 miles downstream from the capital, it was thought that ships would choose to dock there and transfer their goods to the railway rather than make the long journey up the congested River Thames. Fierce competition from the dock companies further upstream meant that Tilbury docks remained empty in the early years and did not make any money for its owners. This problem was resolved in 1908 when the Port of London Authority (PLA) was formed to manage all the London docks together.

By the 1960s the inland docks were too small for the new larger cargo vessels and began to close down. The PLA identified the potential of Tilbury as a deep-water port for attracting large ocean-going ships, and decided to turn it into a modern port. **Container** terminals were built for new container ships to offload their cargoes directly onto trains or trucks. Bulk terminals were built to handle particular goods such as grain, timber and sugar. A special **roll-on, roll-off terminal** allowed trucks to be transported directly across the North Sea to continental Europe without needing to unload their cargoes. Soon Tilbury became one of the most efficient ports in the country. The improved port facilities attracted other industries to the area and Tilbury grew rapidly, as workers and their families moved in to fill the new jobs being created.

1539-40	1588	1667	1670-83
Henry VIII builds the first fort at Tilbury.	Troops camp out by the fort before the Spanish Armada.	Fort is used against the Dutch invasion.	Pentagonal fort with double moat is built.

Dock facilities at Tilbury became highly specialized to cope with the many different cargoes that arrive in the port.

The waterfront at Tilbury is now one of the busiest in the UK, with cranes and ships lining the water's edge and cargoes being sorted and shipped to destinations across the globe. As London's main dock, Tilbury has to keep developing in order to keep up with the demands of the shipping industry. Its container terminal has been extended to cope with the increase in cargo expected in the next few years. New facilities have also been developed to handle goods such as motor vehicles and frozen foods. With such developments it seems that Tilbury is set to remain a key port on the Thames well into the 21st century.

1886	1908	1920
Decision to build a new dock at Tilbury.	Port of London Authority is formed to manage all the London docks together.	Tilbury fort stops being a military garrison.

The Thames of tomorrow

Moving with the times

The **settlements** of the River Thames provide a fascinating glimpse into the history of the British Isles. Today these towns and villages thrive on this history, and millions of tourists visit them each year. The Thames itself has become a major attraction. The London stretch of the Thames alone, attracts over 2 million people on sightseeing cruises every year.

The secret to the success of the Thames and its settlements has been to move with the changing times. Over a period of some two thousand years the river has been transformed from a major transportation route into an industrial waterway and now into a river dominated by leisure and tourism. A symbol of this change is the Tate Modern art gallery, reopened in 2000. It has been built inside the old Bankside power station and is connected to the opposite side of the Thames (near St Paul's Cathedral) by the Millennium Bridge. This is the first free-standing pedestrian bridge to be built across the Thames for over a hundred years.

London has become an attractive tourist destination as an historic and yet modern city.

The Thames looks set to continue as a source of recreation and leisure, but as concerns about the environmental impact of road traffic grow there are some who would like to see the return of river traffic. Many settlements, however, have now turned their old **wharves** and landing sites into luxury homes or leisure complexes. Whether they can again be used for transport is doubtful. Whatever happens in the coming years, the Thames will continue to be Britain's greatest river and to influence the places and the people who live along its banks.

The Thames Path

In 1996 a path linking all the settlements of the Thames from its source to the Thames flood barrier in Woolwich, London was finally completed. The path extends for some 300 km (186 miles) and achieves the goal of creating a path along the Thames that dates back to 1920. It is a unique long-distance path – the only one to follow a river for its entire length.

A picturesque stretch of the Thames Path as it passes through Radcot.

Timeline

AD 43	Romans invade Britain.
50	Wooden bridge is built across the Thames at London by the Romans.
60	Queen Boudica invades London.
100 – 410	Londinium is capital of Britannia.
700	Frideswide founds a monastery near the oxen ford.
1018	King Canute is crowned in Oxford.
1070	William I builds the first fort at Windsor.
1215	**Magna Carta** is signed at Runnymede by King John.
1250	Founding of Maidenhead, with a wooden bridge built across the Thames.
1297	**Wharf** built near Maidenhead's bridge, bringing in trade.
1300s	Religious scholars found the first colleges at Oxford.
1478	Book printing begins in Oxford.
1539 – 40	Henry VIII builds the first fort at Tilbury.
1588	Troops camp out by Tilbury fort before the Spanish Armada.
1666	Great Fire of London, lasting three days.
1667	Tilbury fort is used against the Dutch invasion.
1670 – 83	Pentagonal fort with double moat is built at Tilbury.
1789	Canal link from Lechlade to the River Severn completed.
1790	Oxford canal is completed.
1792	Halfpenny Bridge at Lechlade is constructed.
1824	Iron bridge is built across the Thames at Windsor.
1839	Brunel's 'Sounding Arch Bridge' is built across the Thames at Maidenhead.
1843	Railways arrive in Oxford.
1886	Decision to build a new dock at Tilbury.
1908	Port of London Authority manages all the London docks together.
1920	Tilbury fort stops being a military garrison.
1930	Canal at Lechlade is abandoned.
1939 – 45	Second World War badly damages London's docklands.
1947	One of the worst floods in Windsor.
2003	Jubilee River is used for the first time.

Further resources

Books to read

Rivers of Britain and Ireland (Great Rivers),
Michael Pollard (Evans Brothers, 2002)

The Story of London: From Roman River to Capital City,
Jacqui Bailey and Christopher Maynard (A & C Black 2000)

The Thames (The World's Rivers),
D. Rogers (Hodder Wayland, 1996)

Websites

Environment Agency Thames (www.visitthames.co.uk)
UK Environment Agency website about the Thames and its
settlements. Includes virtual tour of the river.

**London docklands
(www.bardaglea.org.uk/docklands/index.html)**
Look at the history of the London docklands from their origins
to their final closure. Very detailed and highly recommended.

River Thames (www.the-river-thames.co.uk)
A private website run by a couple who have spent many years
exploring the Thames and its settlements. A useful 'Thames
Information' section.

Royal Windsor (www.thamesweb.co.uk)
A very informative site about Windsor, with a section especially
devoted to the Thames at Windsor and the history of its
flooding. Includes many historical images.

Glossary

altitude height above sea level

archaeology investigating the past from evidence that has been left behind, which usually lies buried in the ground

barge narrow , long and flat-bottomed boat used for transporting goods. Some barges are also used to carry people.

berth place where ships can anchor

besiege when a surrounding force traps its enemy and cuts it off from the outside world

blockhouse fort buildings made of timber

bluff a steep hill, mound or cliff

civil war conflict between two groups within one country

coaching town settlement where coaching (wagons drawn by horses) was important

container standard-sized metal box, designed to store goods and be easily transferred between different methods of transport

East and West India Dock Companies two dock companies that played a key role in the development of London's docklands. They were so called because they traded with the East and West Indies.

embankment raised platform or ridge, normally made of earth or stone. Used to keep a river in a particular course.

estuary the lower course of a river where saltwater (from the sea) flows in to mix with freshwater

garrison a military post (building or site) where troops are stationed. Often built in a defensive position.

Industrial Revolution process of technological changes that changed societies and economies in the UK, America and Europe. It began in the UK in the mid-18th century.

lighter small flat-bottomed boat, used for off-loading ocean-going ships. Lighters were widely used to help manage the congested waterways of the Thames in London.

Magna Carta political agreement about the rights of citizens. It was signed by King John at Runnymede (on the Thames) in 1215. The Magna Carta is the basis of British and American law today.

meandering winding from side to side rather than following a direct (straight) route

medieval a period of time in Europe that is also known as the Middle Ages (c.700 – c.1500)

mint place where coins were made

narrow boat shallow barge, built to carry goods along artificial canals. Now a popular form of leisure boat on canals and rivers in the UK.

navigation act of directing or moving a boat along a river or across a lake or sea

province a territory or area of land within an empire

reach part of a river's course. Rivers are normally divided into upper, middle and lower reaches.

roll-on, roll-off terminal a port or dock facility that allows lorries or other vehicles to drive on and off ships without the need to unload their cargoes

Saxons people of Germanic origin who spread westwards into the UK during Roman times. They became the dominant rulers in the UK.

settlement place that has people living in it permanently. Settlements can vary in size from a small village to a large city.

tidal influenced by the rise and fall of the tides

toll a charge against people or goods that is normally made for crossing a bridge

tributary river or stream that joins another, normally larger, river

urban area that is built up with housing, industry and transport networks

water meadows areas of grassland that are frequently flooded by rivers during periods of high flow. They are a natural feature of many rivers.

wharf structure built in a riverbank or out into a river that allows boats to moor and load or unload their cargo

winch machine that uses a rope or chain (wound around a wheel) to hoist or pull things

Index